The INSIDE GUIDE

WOMEN IN U.S. HISTORY

Women in the Fight Against Slavery

By Therese M. Shea

Cavendish Square

Published in 2025 by Cavendish Square Publishing, LLC
2544 Clinton Street Buffalo, NY 14224

First Edition

Website: cavendishsq.com

Library of Congress Cataloging-in-Publication Data

Names: Shea, Therese, author.
Title: Women in the fight against slavery / Therese M. Shea.
Description: New York : Cavendish Square Publishing, [2025] | Series: The inside guide: women in U.S. history | Includes index.
Identifiers: LCCN 2024024990 (print) | LCCN 2024024991 (ebook) | ISBN 9781502673091 (library binding) | ISBN 9781502673084 (paperback) | ISBN 9781502673107 (ebook)
Subjects: LCSH: Women abolitionists–United States–History–Juvenile literature. | Abolitionists–United States–History–Juvenile literature. | Antislavery movements–United States–History–Juvenile literature. | Slavery–United States–History–Juvenile literature.
Classification: LCC E449 .S54 2025 (print) | LCC E449 (ebook) | DDC 326/.8/0973–dc23/eng/20240604
LC record available at https://lccn.loc.gov/2024024990
LC ebook record available at https://lccn.loc.gov/2024024991

Editor: Therese M. Shea
Copyeditor: Danielle Haynes
Designer: Deanna Lepovich

The photographs in this book are used by permission and through the courtesy of: Cover Shutterstock AI Generator/Shutterstock.com; pp. 4, 9, 16, 24, 25, 29 (left) Everett Collection/Shutterstock.com; p. 7 The 1688 Germantown Quaker petition against slavery/Wikimedia Commons; p. 8 (top) duncan1890/iStock.com; p. 8 (bottom) Capture of the Indian Fortress/Wikimedia Commons; pp. 10, 14, 19, 20, 22, 27 courtesy of the Library of Congress; p. 12 Mott Lucretia Painting Kyle 1841/Wikimedia Commons; p. 13 PFASS seal/Wikimedia Commons; p. 15 1840 Anti Slavery/Wikimedia Commons; p. 18 The Underground Railroad by Charles T. Webber, 1893/Wikimedia Commons; p. 21 Laura Haviland OhioHistoryMuseum 001/Wikimedia Commons; p. 26 Nurses during the American Civil War, undated/Wikimedia Commons; p. 29 (right) UncleTomsCabinCover/Wikimedia Commons.

CPSIA compliance information: Batch #CWCSQ25: For further information contact Cavendish Square Publishing LLC at 1-877-980-4450.

Printed in the United States of America

CONTENTS

This is an illustration of enslaved Africans arriving in Point Comfort in today's Virginia in 1619.

SLAVERY IN THE AMERICAN COLONIES

Chapter One

The first enslaved Africans arrived in the North American colonies of England in August 1619. European enslavers transported about 30 people from what is now the African nation of Angola and sold them to settlers. This was about 12 years after the establishment of England's first successful permanent settlement in Jamestown in modern Virginia. The slave trade in North America began, and it would take the efforts of many courageous Americans, including many women, to end slavery on U.S. soil nearly 250 years later.

An American Institution

After the American colonies won their independence from Great Britain in 1783, the United States held on to slavery. However, some

Fast Fact

Some historians classify the first African arrivals as indentured servants rather than enslaved people because most were released after working for a time. However, Europeans kidnapped them from their homeland and forced them to work.

Fast Fact
All U.S. states north of Maryland abolished slavery by 1804.

Northern states began to abolish it, starting with Vermont in 1777.

The agricultural economies of the Southern states, though, were tied to large farms with large workforces. Many Southerners wanted enslaved people to meet their labor needs.

The first U.S. **census** in 1790 showed that there were nearly 700,000 enslaved people in the nation. When slavery was finally abolished throughout the country in 1865, about 3.6 million enslaved people lived in the nation. From 1619 to 1865, an estimated 10 million men, women, and children of African descent had been enslaved in the territory that became the United States.

Fast Fact
Early British colonies weren't the only ones with legalized slavery. Spanish colonizers transported enslaved Africans to the Carolinas in 1526 and to Florida in 1565.

The Background of American Abolitionism

Many Americans didn't enslave others, and many thought slavery was wrong. However, most benefited from slavery in some way and did nothing to stop it. That wasn't true of all Americans, though. In particular, the Christian group called the Quakers, or Society of Friends, came to believe and declare publicly that all people are equal and should be treated as such. Many women who fought against slavery were Quakers.

In the 1700s, the Enlightenment movement spread throughout Europe and the Americas. Enlightenment philosophers, or thinkers,

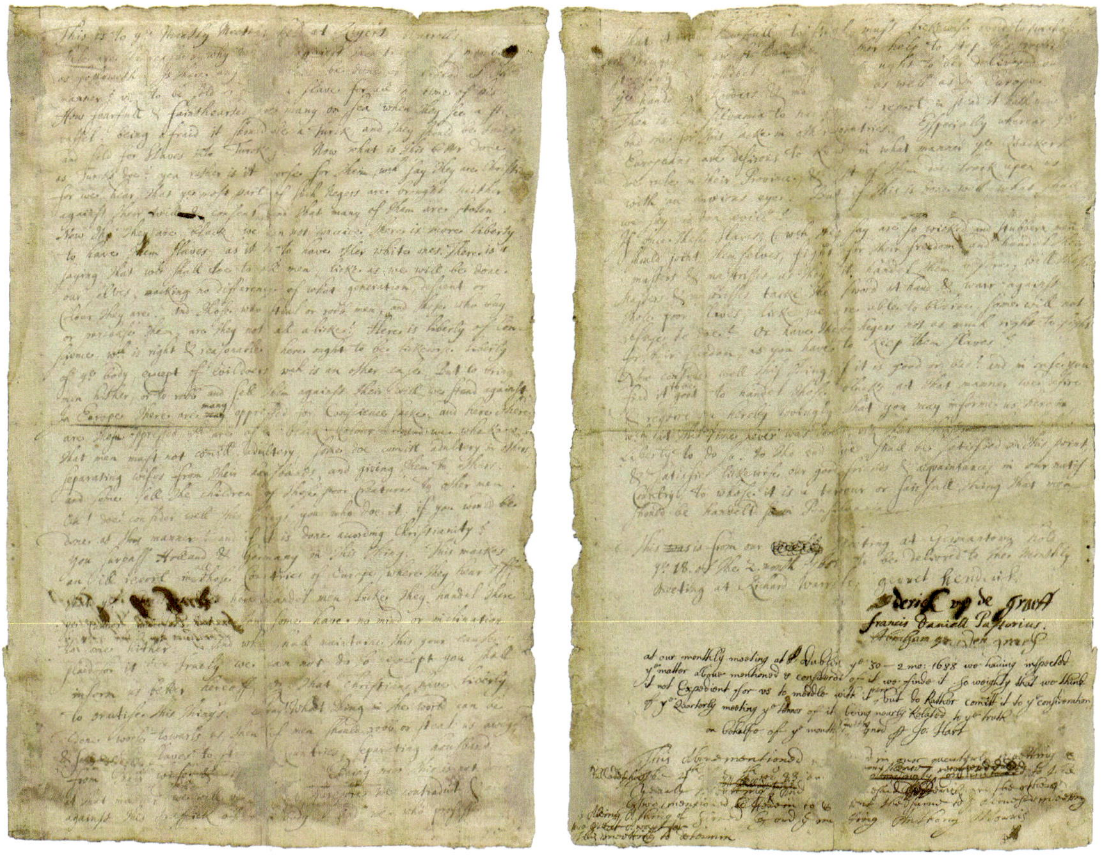

In 1688, four Quakers in today's Philadelphia, Pennsylvania, wrote a petition (shown here) to abolish slavery in their colony, basing their arguments on the Bible. It was largely ignored at the time.

applied reason and science to the world. Many wanted to apply the ideas of equality and other human rights to government and society.

The Abolitionist Movement Begins

By the early 1800s, a growing number of Americans viewed slavery as immoral. The first organized effort to end slavery across the United States began around 1830.

NATIVE AMERICAN SLAVERY

Europeans enslaved Native peoples in the Americas. Christopher Columbus and his crew enslaved the people he encountered in his explorations of the Caribbean. Later, some American colonists forced local Native American groups to work for them, while some sold Native Americans to slave traders who transported them to the Caribbean and beyond. As late as 1850 in California, Native Americans were forced to do labor to pay off debts or fines for crimes. This wasn't called slavery, which was illegal in California, but the Native Americans had to comply. Between 1492 and 1900, as many as 5 million Native Americans had been enslaved.

Christopher Columbus treated the Taíno people of the Caribbean cruelly, enslaving and selling thousands.

Selling Native Americans into slavery was one way colonists removed them from their lands. Colonial leaders sold as many as 1,000 Native Americans into slavery after King Philip's War (1675–1676).

At first, the face of the U.S. abolitionist movement was white, male, and religious, such as William Lloyd Garrison. As the movement gained speed, however, supporters became more diverse, or varied, and included Black Americans. Those who had been enslaved were especially influential. Frederick Douglass, for example, had escaped slavery to become a celebrated antislavery **activist**. Many women, both Black and white, were effective and important as abolitionist leaders too.

The importing of enslaved people ended in the United States in 1808, but the fight to end slavery lasted decades longer. By law, children who were born to enslaved mothers were enslaved.

Women and men worked separately to end slavery at first. This photograph shows Philadelphia abolitionists in 1851.

Chapter Two

ABOLITION SOCIETIES

William Lloyd Garrison, Henry Tappan, and other male abolitionists established the American Anti-Slavery Society in 1833. While women were present and supportive, they weren't allowed to be members.

This group acted as the main abolitionist organization in the United States. Meetings and lectures, or talks, were among its efforts to sway public opinion against slavery. The society also sent petitions to Congress, published journals, and printed antislavery messages. State and local groups operated under the main organization.

Women Take the Lead

Some of the early female supporters of the American Anti-Slavery Society, including Lucretia Mott, wanted a more active role, or part, in the abolitionist movement. About 20 of these women founded the Philadelphia Female Anti-Slavery Society in 1833. This organization, which invited both white and Black women to join, wasn't the only women's

Fast Fact

By 1840, seven years after its founding, the American Anti-Slavery Society had 2,000 smaller groups and up to 200,000 members.

Many people criticized Lucretia Mott, a founding member of the Philadelphia Female Anti-Slavery Society and women's rights activist, for speaking in public. American culture frowned on this behavior at that time.

antislavery group of that time, but it was arguably the most famous. Members worked hard on key issues. For example, they demanded federal areas, such as Washington, D.C., ban slavery.

The Philadelphia Female Anti-Slavery Society organized an antislavery **convention** in 1838, which was attended by women and men, both Black and white. Women were also speakers at this meeting. These features of the convention were rare at that time, and some outsiders disapproved. In fact, an angry mob set the building where they were meeting on fire. The society still held a convention the following year.

Members of the Philadelphia Female Anti-Slavery Society also helped house, protect, and guide people who escaped enslavement. During the American Civil War (1861–1865), members supported the war effort as well as Black Americans' right to vote.

The Philadelphia Female Anti-Slavery Society had large fairs at which they sold baked goods, crafts, and more. Funds raised supported antislavery efforts. The seal of the society, based on that of a British abolition society, is shown here.

A Split in the Society

In 1839, the American Anti-Slavery Society's national organization split in two. One of the main reasons for this was that one part, led by William Lloyd Garrison, wanted to include women in leadership and public-speaking positions. Garrison's group kept the name American Anti-Slavery Society. The group insisting on male leadership became known as the American and Foreign Anti-Slavery Society.

Fast Fact

The Philadelphia Female Anti-Slavery Society had a constitution in which they stated their "abhorrence of the flagrant [obvious] injustice and deep sin of slavery by united and vigorous exertions."

SOJOURNER TRUTH

Sojourner Truth was born Isabella Baumfree in New York around 1797. She was enslaved from birth. In 1827, the year New York abolished slavery, she ran away from her enslavers. An abolitionist family bought her freedom and helped her sue to get back her young son who had been illegally enslaved in the South. She went to New York City, where she became inspired by a religious movement to become a public speaker. She renamed herself Sojourner Truth. Her most famous speech, which she gave at a convention in Akron, Ohio, in 1851, was called "Ain't I a Woman?" She argued for both women's rights and an end to slavery.

Although she never learned to read or write, Sojourner Truth told her life story and had it published in 1850 as *The Narrative of Sojourner Truth*. After the Civil War, she worked with the Freedmen's Bureau, helping formerly enslaved people find jobs.

Fast Fact

Some public speakers in the American Anti-Slavery Society had been enslaved, including Frederick Douglass and Sojourner Truth.

In this painting of the 1840 antislavery convention in London, you can see women pictured, though they weren't allowed to take part.

The World Anti-Slavery Convention was held in London, England, in 1840, bringing together antislavery societies from different countries. However, even though some societies sent women delegates, women weren't allowed to participate.

Women's treatment in the abolitionist movement pushed the women's rights movement forward. It led to women organizing a fight for their rights. Two women at the World Anti-Slavery Convention, Lucretia Mott and Elizabeth Cady Stanton, planned a women's rights convention. It took place in Seneca Falls, New York, eight years later. However, even as these women campaigned for their own rights, they continued the fight to end slavery.

The Fugitive Slave Act of 1850 led to free Black people being captured and enslaved illegally. Under the law, they couldn't speak for themselves in court.

THE UNDERGROUND RAILROAD

Chapter Three

The Fugitive Slave Acts were two laws, passed by Congress in 1793 and 1850. These laws provided for the return of enslaved people who had run away from their enslavers, even if they were found in states that didn't allow slavery. The 1850 act established that people who helped freedom seekers would be punished. In addition, it made the federal government oversee the capture of escaped enslaved people. The law outraged many in the North, increased the number of abolitionists, and made the Underground Railroad more organized and ready to aid freedom seekers than ever before.

On the Railroad

The Underground Railroad was a system of paths, people, and places that aided enslaved people seeking freedom, mainly in the northern U.S. states or Canada. Calling its activities by train terms helped disguise its purpose: The escaping people were "freight" or "passengers," routes were "lines," places to stop were "stations" or "depots," and those who helped along the way were "conductors." In the four decades the Underground Railroad was in operation, an estimated 40,000 to 100,000 people escaped enslavement.

This 1893 painting by Charles T. Webber portrays the Coffin family assisting people on the Underground Railroad. Levi and Catherine Coffin made their Indiana home into a station, helping more than 3,000 freedom seekers.

Female abolitionists were key in helping hide, feed, clothe, and aid people on the Underground Railroad. Some were members of antislavery societies. Others were escaped enslaved people themselves, most notably Harriet Tubman.

General Tubman

Harriet Tubman escaped her lifelong enslavement in Maryland in 1849, when she was about 29 years old. She used the Underground

During the Civil War, Harriet Tubman served as a nurse, cook, scout, and spy. In one mission, she helped rescue hundreds of enslaved people.

Railroad to reach Philadelphia, Pennsylvania. The next year, she made the first of 13 dangerous journeys back to Maryland to lead people north to freedom. She's thought to have rescued about 70 people directly and aided at least another 70 by giving them information about how to use the Underground Railroad.

Tubman famously never left one of her freedom seekers behind. She said, "I was the conductor of the Underground Railroad for eight years, and I can say what most conductors can't say—I never ran my train off the track, and I never lost a passenger."

Fast Fact

After an enslaver injured Harriet Tubman in 1835, she lived with chronic pain and narcolepsy for the rest of her life.

UNCLE TOM'S CABIN

Harriet Beecher Stowe was an author whose most famous work, *Uncle Tom's Cabin*, helped gain support for abolition. She was inspired to write the book after the passage of the Fugitive Slave Act of 1850, angered that the law required American citizens to participate in enslavement. Her sister-in-law urged her to write a book that would "make this whole nation feel what an accursed thing slavery is." *Uncle Tom's Cabin* was published as a **serial** in an abolitionist newspaper, starting in 1851, and then in novel form in 1852. About 300,000 copies were sold in the United States in its first year, and it was outsold only by the Bible in the 1800s.

Besides writing about the horrors of slavery, Harriet Beecher Stowe helped harbor people running from enslavement.

To accomplish this, she was strict, sometimes forcing her passengers along at gunpoint if necessary.

In addition to her work on the Underground Railroad, Tubman was a speaker for both the abolition and women's rights movements. She was so respected by abolitionist John Brown that he called her "General Tubman." Harriet Tubman is the most famous of the Underground Railroad conductors, but the system's success depended on the bravery, intelligence, and compassion of many other women too.

Fast Fact

The Boston Vigilance Committee of Massachusetts helped people seeking freedom from slavery. Black women were members of the group's "Committees of Reception." Because Black women weren't seen as threats, they could meet ships in the harbor and find out if escaped enslaved people were on board so they could aid them.

Laura Smith Haviland was another conductor on the Underground Railroad. After a journey south, she returned with chains, a neck collar, and other tools of enslavers to show the horrors of slavery to the people of Michigan.

Fast Fact

The city of Haviland, Kansas, is named for abolitionist and Underground Railroad conductor Laura Haviland.

Just 39 days after Abraham Lincoln was sworn in as U.S. president in 1861, Southern (Confederate) forces fired at the federal Fort Sumter in South Carolina. This began the American Civil War.

THE CIVIL WAR

Chapter Four

Tensions between the North and the South increased during the 1850s. Abolitionist John Brown led an attack on a federal **arsenal** in Harpers Ferry, Virginia, in 1859. Brown hoped to supply enslaved people with weapons to begin an uprising that would end slavery. Harriet Tubman helped with the plan and was supposed to take part but fell ill. The plan didn't work, however. The government of Virginia executed Brown for treason.

The presidential election of 1860 was the final event that led to civil war. The slavery issue split the Democratic Party in two. This helped Abraham Lincoln of the Republican Party to be elected. Southern states had threatened to secede, or break off, from the country if he won. South Carolina was the first to secede, on December 20, 1860. War broke out between the Confederacy (South) and Union (North) in April 1861.

Fast Fact

The Republican Party formed in 1854 to fight slavery's further spread into new U.S. states.

At Home and on the Battlefield

During the Civil War, women were expected to tend to their

SLAVERY AND THE WAR

At the beginning of the American Civil War, President Lincoln insisted the war wasn't about slavery, but about preserving the United States. As the war continued, though, Lincoln came to believe that enslaved people had to be freed, especially as they were the workforce of the Confederacy. His Emancipation Proclamation went into effect on January 1, 1863, freeing all enslaved people in Confederate-held territory. To make their freedom last and extend emancipation, or freedom, to all, Congress introduced the 13th Amendment, or change, to the U.S. Constitution. This law, **ratified** on December 6, 1865, abolished slavery in the United States.

The Emancipation Proclamation was a wartime measure. It didn't have the power to abolish slavery permanently. The 13th Amendment accomplished this.

homes and children, while their male relatives went off to fight. Women at home found ways to help the war effort, including organizing groups to collect food for soldiers and to provide clothing and blankets.

About 20,000 women—both white and Black—volunteered to work more directly with the Union army, traveling with the soldiers. Many cooked, cleaned, and did laundry, helping keep soldiers healthy and ready to fight.

Although women weren't officially allowed to serve in either the Northern or Southern armies, an estimated 400 became soldiers. This number isn't exact because the women disguised themselves as men. Some were only found out after they were

Without the efforts of women, many more soldiers would have died in the American Civil War from wounds, illnesses, unhealthy conditions, and other problems in military camps.

wounded or fell ill. Others served the whole war.

Fast Fact

Some women served as spies during the war. Harriet Tubman established an entire system of spies, using people who had been enslaved, in South Carolina.

Saving Lives

Thousands of women became nurses, caring for ill and injured soldiers. When the war began, Dorothea Dix was already a well-known activist and expert in the medical field. She was named superintendent of army nurses for the Union army and appointed about 3,000 Union nurses.

Clara Barton decided to become a nurse when Union soldiers were attacked

By the end of the war, nursing was an acceptable profession for women for the first time.

Clara Barton founded the American Red Cross in 1881 to help Americans in times of war and natural disasters.

near her workplace in Baltimore, Maryland. She later became known as the "Angel of the Battlefield" for her care, helping the wounded even while gunfire erupted around her.

The Union won the war in 1865, and as a result, slavery was abolished across the nation. Undoubtedly, women played a large role in these victories. Their part in the fight against slavery should be forever remembered and honored in U.S. history.

Fast Fact

Before the American Civil War, male doctors provided most medical care, though women were commonly midwives. The number of wounded during the war created a need for women nurses.

A TIMELINE OF U.S. SLAVERY AND ABOLITION

1790
The first U.S. census reports almost 700,000 enslaved people.

1808
The importation of enslaved people ends officially in the United States.

1833
The American Anti-Slavery Society is established. Women are refused membership. The Philadelphia Female Anti-Slavery Society is then established.

1839
The American Anti-Slavery Society splits over the issue of women in leadership.

1849
Harriet Tubman escapes slavery and becomes a leader on the Underground Railroad.

1850
The Fugitive Slave Act allows Black Americans, enslaved and free, to be captured in Northern states.

1852
Harriet Beecher Stowe's story *Uncle Tom's Cabin* is published as a novel.

1859
John Brown's attack on an arsenal in Harpers Ferry, Virginia, fails.

1860
Abraham Lincoln is elected U.S. president. South Carolina is the first state to secede.

1861
The American Civil War begins at Fort Sumter in April.

1863
On January 1, the Emancipation Proclamation frees enslaved people in Confederate territory.

1865
The Civil War ends. The 13th Amendment is ratified, abolishing slavery.

THINK ABOUT IT!

1. Why do you think the enslavement of Native Americans isn't as well known as that of African Americans?
2. Would you label the first Africans who arrived near Jamestown in 1619 and were later freed as enslaved or indentured? Why?
3. How might the abolition movement have been different if women had been allowed to take part as equals from the beginning?
4. Why do you think a fiction book like *Uncle Tom's Cabin* had such a powerful impact on the fight against slavery?

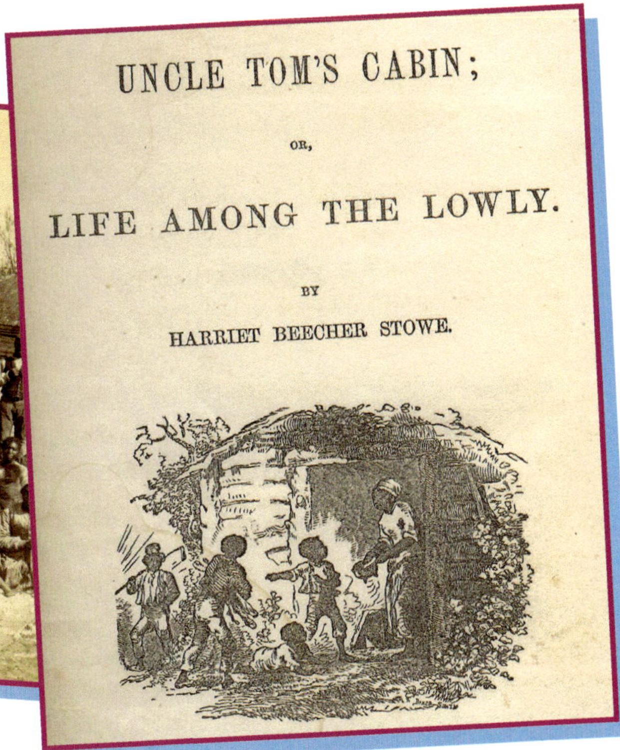

UNCLE TOM'S CABIN;

OR,

LIFE AMONG THE LOWLY.

BY

HARRIET BEECHER STOWE.

GLOSSARY

abhorrence: A feeling of dislike or disgust.

activist: A person who uses or supports strong actions to help make changes in politics or society.

arsenal: A place where weapons are stored.

census: The official process of counting a number of people and collecting information about them.

chronic: Describing something that happens continuously or again and again.

convention: A gathering of people who have a common interest or purpose.

culture: The beliefs and ways of life of a group of people.

indentured servant: One who signs a contract agreeing to to be bound to work for someone for a time in exchange for specific benefits.

midwife: One whose job is to help women and children during birth.

narcolepsy: A condition that causes someone to suddenly fall asleep during activities.

petition: A written request signed by many people asking the government to take an action.

ratify: To formally approve.

serial: Something published in parts over time.

FIND OUT MORE

Books

Blaisdell, Robert, ed. *Female Abolitionists: Phillis Wheatley, Sarah Mapps Douglass, Lydia Maria Child, Harriet Tubman, Elizabeth Cady Stanton, and Others*. Garden City, NY: Dover Publications, 2021.

Stanchak, John E. *Eyewitness Civil War*. New York, NY: DK Publishing, 2023.

Taylor, Whit. *Harriet Tubman: Toward Freedom*. New York, NY: Little, Brown and Company, 2021.

Websites

BKBB: Women and the Anti-slavery Movement (1830s)
bkbbphilly.org/source-set/women-and-anti-slavery-movement-1830s
Read more about women in the early years of the U.S. abolition movement.

***National Geographic*: Key Figures of the Abolitionist Movement**
education.nationalgeographic.org/resource/key-figures-abolitionist-movement/
Learn more about the lives and legacies of Sojourner Truth, Harriet Tubman, and Frederick Douglass.

PBS: Abolition and Suffrage
www.pbs.org/kenburns/not-for-ourselves-alone/abolition-suffrage
Find out more about how the movement for women's suffrage was rooted in the fight against slavery.

INDEX